D1607016

Rescues in Focus
Storm Rescues

by Mark L. Lewis

FOCUS
READERS

BEACON

www.focusreaders.com

Focus Readers is distributed by North Star Editions:
sales@northstareditions.com | 888-417-0195

Produced for Focus Readers by Red Line Editorial.

Photographs ©: David J. Phillip/AP Images, cover, 1; Steve Helber/AP Images, 4; Atilgan Ozdil/Anadolu Agency/Getty Images, 7; Chris Seward/AP Images, 8; Petty Officer 3rd Class Ross Ruddell/US Coast Guard, 10; Petty Officer 1st Class Chuck Ferrante/US Coast Guard/Defense Visual Information Distribution Service, 13; Anirut Ruairuen/Shutterstock Images, 15; Chip Somodevilla/Getty Images News/Getty Images, 17, 29; Cai zirong/Imaginechina/AP Images, 18–19; gdagys/iStockphoto, 20; Petty Officer 1st Class Brandyn Hill/Defense Visual Information Distribution Service, 23; Ramon Espinosa/AP Images, 25; Fred Lancelot/AP Images, 27 (people); MarioGuti/iStockphoto, 27 (boat)

Library of Congress Cataloging-in-Publication Data
Names: Lewis, Mark L., 1991- author.
Title: Storm rescues / by Mark L. Lewis.
Description: Lake Elmo, MN : Focus Readers, [2020] | Series: Rescues in focus | Audience: Grade 4 to 6. | Includes bibliographical references and index.
Identifiers: LCCN 2019008695 (print) | LCCN 2019011681 (ebook) | ISBN 9781641859813 (pdf) | ISBN 9781641859127 (ebook) | ISBN 9781641857741 (hardcover) | ISBN 9781641858434 (pbk.)
Subjects: LCSH: Rescue work--Juvenile literature. | Natural disasters--Juvenile literature.
Classification: LCC HV553 (ebook) | LCC HV553 .L488 2020 (print) | DDC 363.34/92181--dc23
LC record available at https://lccn.loc.gov/2019008695

Printed in the United States of America
Mankato, MN
May, 2019

About the Author

Mark L. Lewis lives in Minnesota but has traveled all over the world. He loves writing books for young readers.

Table of Contents

Chapter 1

Hurricane Florence

A hurricane hit the eastern United States in 2018. In North Carolina, the town of New Bern flooded. This town lies between two rivers. When those rivers overflowed, the water rushed into the town.

 More than 16 inches (41 cm) of rain fell on New Bern during Hurricane Florence.

The flood rose to 10 feet (3.0 m) within hours.

Volunteer rescuers David Rouse and Christopher Hawkins helped save people in New Bern. They used a boat to travel around the flooded town. They had to avoid the tops of cars and fences. They even had to

Did You Know?

Meteorologists in New Bern had to quickly leave their news station. It flooded during the storm.

 Firefighters use a boat to assist flood victims in New Bern.

watch out for alligators swimming in the water.

Rouse and Hawkins made approximately 15 rescue trips in two hours. They rescued one man who was trapped in his apartment.

More than 1,200 people had to leave their homes in New Bern due to the hurricane.

Rouse and Hawkins used a cooler to help the man onto the boat. The cooler acted as a stepping stone.

Rouse and Hawkins also rescued a family of 12 people. The family had garbage bags filled with important things. Rouse and Hawkins rescued all 12 family members. They needed two trips to take the whole family to safety.

The storm ruined homes, stores, and cars. But rescuers saved at least 360 people in the town.

Did You Know?

During Hurricane Florence, a retired Marine used his army truck to rescue people in New Bern.

Chapter 2

Becoming a Rescuer

Many different people act as rescuers during a storm. Some are volunteers. Other rescuers are part of the military. For example, the US Coast Guard helps with storm rescues.

 On average, the US Coast Guard saves 10 lives every day.

Training for the US Coast Guard is eight weeks long. Some **recruits** learn to control boats in fast water. Others learn to fly a helicopter in one place. Then, rescuers can help the victim up.

Some recruits train to become rescue swimmers. First they go through basic training. Then they train for 24 more weeks. Recruits practice swimming in pools with wind machines. These machines **simulate** hurricane winds.

 During training, a helicopter hovers in place as a rescue swimmer drops into the water.

Rescue swimmers also learn how to safely help victims. People trapped in water can be afraid. They can hurt rescuers by accident. So trainers pretend to be scared victims. They splash in the water.

They try to climb onto the rescue swimmer. The rescue swimmer learns to stay calm.

Floodwaters sometimes move fast. So, rescuers also learn how to help people caught in floods. These rescues are called swift water rescues. First, rescuers need

Did You Know?

Between 2005 and 2014, rescuers made more than 3,000 swift water rescues in Texas.

 Workers often use ropes and stretchers during swift water rescues.

to **assess** the situation. They must find a good place to attempt the rescue. In many cases, they can enter the water from a bridge.

Swift water rescuers also learn about different **flotation** devices.

One common flotation device is called a rescue can. A rescue can has handles. It is plastic and hollow. Victims hold on to the handles. Rescuers tow the person to safety.

Volunteers may have less training than professionals. But some volunteers are retired rescuers.

Did You Know?

The Cajun Navy is a volunteer rescue group in the United States. During a 2017 hurricane in Texas, one volunteer rescued 153 people in three hours.

> **A volunteer helps rescue a girl after a hurricane flooded her family's home.**

They need to use their own tools.
Some volunteers travel hundreds of
miles. Professionals and volunteers
work together to get people
to safety.

Flooding in China

A **typhoon** hit eastern Asia in 2018. The storm's rain caused problems for more than 1.2 million people in China. Approximately 127,000 victims had to evacuate. But many people weren't able to leave. Floods had trapped them in their homes.

The local fire department sent 300 people to help victims. The department ordered 100 more rescuers to be ready. After 10 hours, rescuers had saved more than 7,000 people who were trapped by floods. By the end of the day, rescuers had helped more than 55,000 people.

China faces some of the worst floods on Earth.

Chapter 3

On the Job

Big storms often bring a lot of rain. Floods can happen within hours. These events are called flash floods. In some cases, victims may be unable to get to safety. These people need rescuers.

 During floods, people will use anything to get to safety. One couple in Thailand used foam as a raft.

Rescue teams study the flood. They decide how to reach flood victims safely. In deep water they use boats. They may use trucks in shallow water. Sometimes, neither a truck nor a boat can reach a victim. In that case, the rescue team may use a helicopter.

Rescuers in boats wear life jackets. They often bring extra life jackets for the victims. High winds can send branches and other objects flying. For this reason,

 Rescue swimmers often use rescue hoists to lift themselves up to helicopters.

rescuers also wear helmets. Many

rescuers wear dry suits, too.

These suits keep rescuers dry

and warm if they enter the water.

Gloves are also helpful. They have better grip than bare hands.

Sometimes, it is not safe for rescuers to go to the victim. Teams might bring ropes if water is moving too fast. Victims can hang on to the rope. Then they can pull themselves to safety.

Did You Know?

In 2013, firefighters saved workers in China. Workers hung on to a rope above a flood. The water carried their trucks away a few seconds later.

During a flood, a man grabs a rope to reach safety.

Radios help rescuers talk to one another. **Dispatchers** find victims' locations through their phones.

Then dispatchers use radios to tell rescuers where to go.

Rescuers also carry whistles. Victims listen for these whistles. They shout for help if they hear one. Then rescuers can find those victims. Other rescuers can also hear the whistle if one of them gets separated.

If the victims are hurt, rescuers take them to the hospital. If the victims are not hurt, rescuers may take them to a shelter. People can

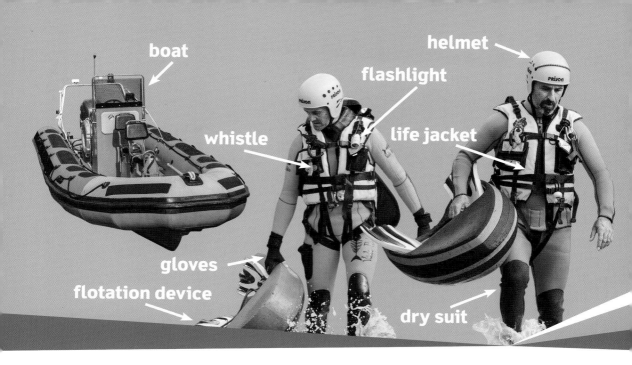

boat

helmet

flashlight

whistle

life jacket

gloves

flotation device

dry suit

eat at the shelter. They can put on dry clothes. A shelter is also a dry place to sleep during storms.

A storm can put many lives at risk. Rescuers use their skills and tools when storms come. They work to help as many victims as they can.

FOCUS ON
Storm Rescues

Write your answers on a separate piece of paper.

1. Write a letter to a friend describing what tools a storm rescuer might need.

2. Would you want to be a volunteer rescuer during a storm? Why or why not?

3. Who rescued the flood victims in China?
   - **A.** volunteers
   - **B.** the fire department
   - **C.** the Coast Guard

4. Why might volunteer rescuers have less training than other rescuers?
   - **A.** Volunteers are naturally skilled rescuers.
   - **B.** Volunteers have other jobs that take up their time.
   - **C.** Volunteers care less about training than others.

5. What does **swift** mean in this book?

*Floodwaters sometimes move fast. So, rescuers also learn how to help people caught in floods. These rescues are called **swift** water rescues.*

    A. unsafe
    B. deep
    C. fast

6. What does **evacuate** mean in this book?

*Approximately 127,000 victims had to **evacuate.** But many people weren't able to leave.*

    A. to leave an area
    B. to stay at home
    C. to rescue others

Answer key on page 32.

Glossary

assess
To judge the conditions of something.

dispatchers
Emergency responders who take phone calls from people who need help.

flotation
The ability to not sink in a liquid.

meteorologists
Scientists who study the weather.

recruits
New members of a group.

simulate
To create an imitation of something.

typhoon
A hurricane, usually near Japan, China, or Southeast Asia.

volunteer
A person who helps without being paid.

To Learn More

BOOKS

Bell, Samantha S. *Detecting Hurricanes*. Lake Elmo, MN: Focus Readers, 2017.

Felix, Rebecca. *Hurricane Harvey: Disaster in Texas and Beyond*. Minneapolis: Lerner Publications, 2018.

Waeschle, Amy. *Daring Flood Rescues*. North Mankato, MN: Capstone Press, 2018.

NOTE TO EDUCATORS

Visit **www.focusreaders.com** to find lesson plans, activities, links, and other resources related to this title.

Index

B
boats, 6, 8, 12, 22, 27

D
dispatchers, 25–26
dry suits, 23, 27

F
fire departments, 18
floods, 6, 14, 18,
    21–22, 24

H
helicopters, 12, 22
helmets, 23, 27
hospitals, 26
hurricanes, 5, 9, 12, 16

L
life jackets, 22, 27

R
radios, 25–26
rescue cans, 16
rescue swimmers, 12–14
ropes, 24

S
shelters, 26–27
swift water rescues,
    14–15

T
typhoons, 18

U
US Coast Guard, 11–12

V
volunteers, 6, 11, 16–17

W
whistles, 26–27

Answer Key: 1. Answers will vary; **2.** Answers will vary; **3.** B; **4.** B; **5.** C; **6.** A